CARL EDWARDS

Nicole Pristash

PowerKiDS
press

New York

Published in 2009 by The Rosen Publishing Group, Inc.
29 East 21st Street, New York, NY 10010

First Edition

Book Design: Michael J. Flynn
Layout Design: Kate Laczynski
Photo Researcher: Jessica Gerweck

Photo Credits: Cover, pp. 5–7, pp. 11–21 © Getty Images, Inc.; p. 9 © AP Images.

Library of Congress Cataloging-in-Publication Data

Pristash, Nicole.
  Carl Edwards / Nicole Pristash. — 1st ed.
      p. cm. — (NASCAR champions)
  Includes index.
  ISBN 978-1-4042-4449-8 (library binding) ISBN 978-1-4042-4545-7 (pbk)
  ISBN 978-1-4042-4563-1 (6-pack)
  1. Edwards, Carl, 1979– 2. Stock car drivers—United States—Biography—Juvenile literature. I. Title.
  GV1032.E36P75 2009
  796.72092—dc22
  [B]
                                    2007047935

Manufactured in the United States of America

Contents

Carl Edwards is a NASCAR driver. He learned about racing from his father, who was also a race car driver.

4

Carl learned to drive when he was 14 years old. He practiced on small race cars called mini sprints.

6

In 2002, Carl's **career** began in NASCAR's Craftsman Truck **Series**. Many race car drivers start out driving trucks.

8

9

Carl soon began racing cars for the Busch Series and Nextel Cup Series, now called the Sprint Cup Series. His Sprint Cup racing number is 99.

In 2005, Carl became the first driver ever to win a Busch Series race and Nextel Cup race in the same weekend.

Carl Edwards gets very **excited** when he wins races. He is known for doing **backflips** off his car!

14

15

In 2007, Carl became one of the point leaders in NASCAR's **rankings**. A driver gets 185 points when he wins a race.

17

Carl likes to play guitar in his free time. He even owns his own music **company**, called Back40 Records.

18

Carl Edwards has become one of NASCAR's best new drivers. This **champion** hopes to get even better and win a lot more races!

21

Glossary

backflips (BAK-flips) Tricks in which people spin upside down in the air.

career (kuh-REER) A job.

champion (CHAM-pee-un) The best, or the winner.

company (KUMP-nee) A group of people who turn out goods or services.

excited (ik-SYT-ed) Having interest.

rankings (RAN-kingz) Guides to how well a player is doing in a sport.

series (SIR-eez) A group of races.

Books and Web Sites

Books

Cavin, Curt. *Under the Helmet: Inside the Mind of a Driver.* Mankato, MN: The Child's World, 2003.

Riley, Gail Blasser. *NASCAR Rules.* Blazers, 2008.

Web Sites

Due to the changing nature of Internet links, the Rosen Publishing Group, Inc., has developed an online list of Web sites related to the subject of this book. This site is updated regularly. Please use this link to access the list: www.powerkidslinks.com/nascar/edwards/

Index